TIME AND TIDE

A Christian Poetry Collection

by Ray Martin

Adrift on the Tide

Wave after wave rolls into the shore.
Plumes of clouds are painted on the horizon.
Whitecaps of rolling breakers are whiter than
The clouds that blend into the pastel blue.

Drifting from a chair
Into the emerald swells before me,
I float out like a soaring seagull
To ride on the currents beneath.

Floating beneath the summer sky,
I'm looking back at buildings on the shore.
Within the rush of wind and salty waves,
I'm released from where I was before.

My mind is so far away
From the distant plains and valleys of the past.
Adrift on the tide, this abandonment
Carries me to a sense of being home at last.

After All

For so long, I was sailing
And praying to the Lord
That He'd bring me to the shore.

Then, one day I looked down,
And all around sunlight sparkled in the sand,
And I reached out for your hand.

You know I'll always be there when you call.
I guess some things were meant to last forever after all.

Far beyond this fleeting moment,
When this day is gone—
Our love will go on.
As we travel down this road,
There's one thing I know—
We'll be together wherever we go.
Even when this song ends,
The music really just begins.
And I'll hold you through it all
And always love you, my dear friend.

We've been traveling down this road,
And we've come so far.
And now here we are.

We're standing hand-in-hand,
Looking down this road ahead,
And we'll be together 'til the end.

I know you'll always be there when I call.
I guess some things were meant to last forever after all.

Afternoon Nap

The steady hum of the sound machine drowns
out the sounds of the world outside. The closed curtains
shut out most of the sunlight, so that the room
is only barely lit by the dim light along its fringes.
Lying on the cool, hardwood floor, I watch my daughter
in the shadows of the slats of her crib,
slowly drifting to sleep for her afternoon nap.
The breeze of the air conditioning blankets
my daughter and me, as we lie in the cool darkness.
The breeze of vents and static of the sound machine
muddles her pink, elephant paci's subtle squeak,
as her tiny fingers tinker with the stuffed elephant.
Layered beneath Frozen, frog, and butterfly-covered
blankets, she's surrounded and comforted
by her stuffed animals. Unexpectedly, I feel
a sudden dampness on the sides of my neck
and t-shirt collar. I self-consciously realize
it's from tears that have rolled in trickling streams
from pools welling up around my eyes.
My chest begins to heave, as I cry quietly
And freely now. My mind revisits moments
like these with my other children from years gone by—
holding them on my lap, singing nursery songs,
or saying a prayer before tucking them in.
I'm all-too aware of how quickly these hours
and days slip away, out of touch and gone.
In this still, small moment, another passes
right before us. Though time like sand sifts through
our fingers, I'll savor each moment here with you.

After The Fall

T'wards a mortuary's wooden back door,
Death's bony hand motions to you and me.
Fallen leaves clothe the wintry forest floor.
The whisp'ring wind beckons to creaking trees.
Shadows lengthen in the darkening wood—
The gray veil of snow-filled clouds encroaching.
One more brittle leaf detaches for good;
Circling down, the ground it is approaching.
The barren trees in the sleeping orchard
Have no ripened apples now to eat.
Snow will cloak cracked tendrils in the garden
And rest on chilled, brown apples near my feet.
Barren limbs are raised to the sky by frozen trees.
Soon, they'll be clothed with snow like you and me.

Alone Below the Night

Alone below the night, painted that way for us to see,
This canvas speaks of and to our inmost yearnings.
The layout consists of millions of points of light
Scattered amidst infinite darkness—
Here, but yet so far...
Further than we know.
We can't know— not now...
Maybe never.
Looking out from a rocky shoreline,
Where frigid, wind-blown water laps
Unrhythmically against the boulders—
Things are not as I perceive them,
Nor remotely what I imagine them to be.
So singular am I and finite!
I plummet helplessly short of grasping what I gaze into,
As I catch a mere glimpse of the infinite heavens.
Squinting into the brisk, night air through my lone portal,
My wonder barely plinks a ripple in the vast black.
As I stare out into everything, I am nothing.
Endless volumes of space lie untapped and uncharted,
In sight but fading fast over light years—
Forever reaching and totally unreachable.
Comprehension slips away fast with escaping clouds,
Which seem to be running from beneath countless stars,
Peering in upon a short-lived planet.

Along the Moonlit Shore

What are the whispered words that rise
From the waves and sift through the door?
Feels like they echo the moments gone by,
All of the years passed long before.

As I wander along the moonlit shore,
I don't feel alone out here at all.
Because, God, I know You're right here with me,
And You hear my spirit's call.

How do You hear my every heartbeat
And cry with every tear that I've cried?
Why, for the life of someone like me,
Did You send Your Son to the cross to die?

Why do I doubt You so very often?
And why do I flee from Your gaze?
How do I dare to pose these questions,
When You've carried me all of my days?

How do You know my every thought,
When I seem to forget what I just said?
Sauntering alone beneath the ethereal night,
It shakes my soul that You rose from the dead!

You hold me when tornadoes swirl through my life.

You're my only source of peace.
You gave us a glimpse of the life to come,
And I wonder how it's going to be.

I've got so many things to ask you God,
And I know You'll tell me some day.
I can't wait to be with You in heaven,
Where forever I will stay.

At the Park

Oh, it was a day of bliss,
As I strolled through the greens of the park,
Navigating plump hillsides
Until shadows gave way to the dark.

In sync with the roll of the open fields,
Wandering along roads of cobblestone,
Each bud and blossom mirrored my own breath.
Nature leapt forth with a pulse of its own.

Brittle leaves, which clothed tufts of grass
Like a mother's delicately-knitted shawl,
Swirled into a play of yellows and reds,
Before the wind gently let them fall.

On a ledge above the gardens, I eyed the rush
Of a waterfall, as it plummeted into pools below.
I watched a train cut through the distant hillside,
Only leaving behind remnants of an echo.

With castles perched on the banks of the lawns,
Sweet aromas drifted from flowers in the breeze.
Tucked inside a weathered, stone gazebo,
I watched patterns of birds spring forth from trees.

Climbing to the top of a towering magnolia,

My eyes surveyed the rolling greens below.
My senses flooded with the elation of that view,
In a moment I will forever know.

Oh, it was a day of bliss,
As I strolled through the greens of the park!
Alas, I steered my path homeward,
As the shadows gave way to the dark.

Augusta

The rolling landscape is crowned with magnolias
And clothed in a jacket of green.
Powder-white sand glows like moonlight
Collected in pools far below those heavenly beams.

Pink and white azaleas on the fringes of the green
Are framed by the silent, watching pines.
Around the club grounds, the patrons are lit up,
Glowing like cigars beneath the stars in the spring sky.

Dressed to impress, the patrons swarm about the greens.
Like a flipped switch, the buzz gives way to hush.
As the golfer prepares to hit his shot in silence,
The wind cuts through the tall pines in a hissing rush.

Then, flashing in the sun, the swinging iron
Launches the ball toward a clear, blue sky.
An arcing, white ball, an unearthed clump of sod,
A rustling of fans shift to watch the ball soar by.

Returning to the earth, the ball begins to roll,
Releasing toward the hole. On a wave of green blades,
Breaking down a slope on the edge of the green,
To within just four feet where it stays.

The applause has faded into an echo now,
As the sun sinks beneath the treetops into the night.
On the thirteenth hole beneath whispering pines,
We pause to savor one last view in the soft moonlight.

Beyond the Train Tracks

I used to sit in the evening and look along
The skyline that stretched out beyond the train tracks,
As the lights of buildings slowly welcomed in the coming
night. With this view from on top of the steps by the street,
I'd reflect on the city & life I'd left behind, when I'd make
My way each day among the buildings towering downtown.
Then, thinking back to the streets and cities of Europe,
I'd revisit those sights and glimpses from the past...
Far across the starlit ocean, yet so near in my mind. Looking
out over the train track-branded bridge,
Which passed right over the street, I'd reminisce
On fragments of moments from the distant past.
Staring out beyond the bridge and smoking embers,
The city lights across the night would kindle visions
Of the future, while the moment held me in its gaze.
Tonight, my thoughts revisit those visions
Along a downtown train track,
Amid the blinking lights of the fireflies.
Hearing the distant echo of a passing train,
I see the lamp light's glimmer in my son's eyes,
As we sit beneath sloping tree limbs, underneath
The evening stars stretched out over this summer night.

Blackbird

Hey, little blackbird, up on a wire
Looking down at me,
The way you tilt your head triggers my muse.
When you look at me, what do you see?

As I survey the artistry of winter clouds
Carving out some exotic world far above,
Why can't I sling my spirit up there to soar forever,
In a tapestry that whispers secrets of God's love?

The shadows that sneak along the fringes
Of my psyche always wilt away out here.
Gazing into the brilliant eyes of this scene,
My heart floods with light because the Artist is near.

Considering my own, pounding chest,
As I catch a breath in the midst of this run—
To this miracle, I've grown so numb.
But You brush my realization, and I'm undone.

Still, like a leaking faucet rusts a sink,
Poisonous thoughts often seep into my soul.
Why must my sinful nature thrust a saber in the side
Of my Savior, who makes me whole?

When I think of all the thoughts You know of,

How do You keep a clear mind?
Amid a myriad of forces in the next dimension,
You are the only source of peace I can find.

Our very orbit around the sun is at Your fingertips.
You set the scales of gravity and pull the tides.
You hold the fibers of the universe together.
You're the One who gives each heartbeat of our lives.

You know each and every soul before its conception.
Oh, how great a God you must be!
I'm but a vapor in the face of Your magnitude.
In the midst of Your creation, thanks for making me.

My wonder only spirals upward from here.
Tell me, little blackbird, is this all absurd?
Wait! Why am I talking to you? Though
Aloft, up above the road, you're only a bird.

Breath of God

Breath of God. In this mountain air.
Its sound moves me deep in my soul!
Same breath that brought the world to be,
Through the peaks and valleys, makes clouds roll.

Sent on the wind's whispers and gusts,
These tones rise and become a hush.
Some issue forth as if to speak
Heaven's words on this mountain peak.

Clouds drift slowly by mountainsides,
Past many hues of blues and greens...
On God's breath, which brought life to man
—Eternal life to the redeemed.

The wind moves like The Spirit, who
Spoke His Holy Word into scrolls.
If mountains crumbled to the sea,
God's Word would never cease to be.

A sudden, crisp rush of breeze wafts
A campfire's smoke scent from below.
The same hands that carved these mountains
Brings forth a cold, trickling stream's flow.

Winding trail of damp, well-worn leaves
Guides my descent to lower heights.

One last gaze from an overlook
Fills my heart and soul with these sights.

By the Seashore

Familiar sounds and sensations revisit me,
Here by the seashore with summer drifting in.
The tide's lull drowns the sounds of the motors
Down the waterway with the daylight growing dim.

A seaside painting on the wall depicts a scene,
Which vaguely reflects life somewhere out by the sea.
It transports us away from the things of man—
An impression of the way things used to be.

The rhythmic croaking of the buoy in the channel,
Flooding with the buzz of cicadas in the trees,
Signals the ever-ticking hands of time,
And my mind drifts upon a stream of memories.

Each year, I see how the kids have grown and changed.
In these moments here now, I reminisce,
Treasuring the glimpses of years gone by—
Memories in my heart carved out in permanence.

Coffee Shop

Gentle melodies play on my senses,
As the brisk, night air presses to the window.
Alone amid the chatter that I hear,
I long for the moments when you're near.

Another cigarette melts into smoke, as
Artsy images swirl along the brick walls.
The light from my candle reflects off a pool of wax.
The moon finds me wishing you were back.

I glance at all the faces around the room
And sense a subtle longing in their eyes.
Was it on a whim that they drifted here tonight?
Do they know of God's love like stars across the sky?

I hear a train rolling through the night outside,
As time beats on through the not-so-still dark.
Floating in a stagnant pond of indifferent hearts,
My love for you only deepens when we're apart.

In the light of all eternity,
We've only paused for a brief eclipse.
How I long to hold you for another moment,
Before time like sand slips through our fingertips.

There's still a lot of coffee in my cup;

The rich aroma rises in the air.
I'll stay here alone just a while longer,
'Til I slip through the door into the night with you.

Crossing a Field at the Farm

My thoughts for now find some solace,
Drifting effortlessly to many yesterdays.
Though the wheels of time spin so fast,
I'm seeping deep into the soil of the past.

I meander across a field at the farm—
The tidewater soil soft under foot.
My eyes follow the lay of the landscape
Beneath a deep-blue sky where birds float.

Sweat glistens on my temples in the sunlight.
Scent of *off!* and smell of grass blend in the breeze.
I can still hear tracks from old cassettes,
Like Rush's "Middletown Dreams," in my memories.

Deep through the woods, walking with my dad,
We arrive at a creek— cool on a bed of sand.
We find an old Crush bottle as a keepsake,
But it's these moments together we treasure on this land.

Attached to this farmland, I find my roots here,
Though I've been uprooted and planted elsewhere.
The echoes of centuries of yesterdays
Fill the woods, open fields, and country air.

As I walk along a shaded edge of the woods,
From a limb, a bobwhite sends his refrain.
Carried along on a stirring of the wind
Is the whistle of a distant, passing train.

Soybeans stretch out before me in rows,
Over fields marked with corncob remains.
Time and tide have reshaped the world around us,
But out here— so much remains unchanged.

Dust of Snow

I cannot count the times I've fallen asleep
While talking to You late at night.
But Your presence there in the twilight hours
Issues my spirit starward to take flight.

And there's a silence that comes to a house
When the dust of snow begins to settle all around.
I push back the curtain and peer outside
And watch the pines catch it, as it drifts down.

One can't help but utter a sigh at that view,
As the feathered white sifts by the lamplight afar.
In that moment, we suspend the dispositions
That cloud our conception of who we are.

Echoes from the Playground

Across the school yard, there's an emptiness now.
Echoes of children's voices seem to ring out
but slowly fade into a hush.
A solitary leaf's blown out of touch.
A sudden replay of a moment from those days
gradually shifts into a faded haze
of revisited memories
and impressions, so deep inside of me.
These imprints, sifted beneath the surface by time's
passage, lie somewhere beneath the procession
of these events... though unapparent.
The empty bench beneath the branching trees,
where I watched the kids play, looks out across a field
toward the empty swings in the distance...
reflecting the childhood playground of my own,
receding further into the distant echoes of the fading past.
Oh, the days of life seem to go so fast.

Engulfed in Waves

Where the ocean meets the sky,
A moving painting of sea and cloud
Transports my mind and spirit
Beyond this world, engulfed in waves that crash down.

Flickering light and sparkles dancing—
Imagination and wonder are released!
Varying hues and shapes in the clouds
Carry whispers of places far beyond the sky and sea.

Liquid sand filters through embedded rocks,
Trickling saltwater through the shoals.
Memory and spirit glow like embers
Beneath the fading light, before the ocean's ebb and flow.

The tidal pools along the shoreline
Gather remnants of the life beneath the sea.
Collecting in temporary worlds upon the sand,
They give tiny creatures a place to live out their destiny.

The rippling surface reflects the skies above
And mirrors the pulse of the deep.
I pass by the pier, with its pilings' wavering, dark
Reflections reaching down and out into the roaring sea.

Every Moment

It seems like every color's in your eyes,
And the stars are aligned in your gaze.
As the sunlight gathers in your hair,
I forget about the selfish goals I've chased.
And I'd give up all the world
To see the moonlight on your face!

Every moment I'm with you,
All I've hoped for is coming true.
The visions in the sunrise
Are flooding inside our hearts.
The reflection's in our eyes—
Slowly bringing together
Two lives that were once apart.

When it's just you and me, we're not alone
Because God in heaven is on His throne.
His Spirit in our hearts draws us together.
He'll be watching over us now and forever.

And I know, wherever we go,
There'll always be so much that we just don't know.
But, if we keep our eyes on the skies above,
Our hearts will be united by God's grace and love.

Far Beyond the Ocean

Walking tonight under the starlight,
Out past the lights of the pier —
With the waves that rush in, I feel my thoughts ascend,
And I know that You're here.

With the glimmering reflections on the ocean,
I ponder Your mystery.
Though worlds separate me from who You are,
You still condescend to me.

Far beyond the ocean... far beyond the sea,
Jesus walked across the water to rescue me.
Over the sands shifting through time,
By the castles on the shore —
You lead me way out, far beyond
All I've ever known before.

My eyes follow the lights on the coast
That silhouette the shoreline.
But behold, more so, the starry host,
Far above that outlasts a lifetime.

As weathered wood drifts in, I feel
Your Spirit descend to help me find the way.
You lead me in between a world of restless dreams
And the dawning of the day.

Now, I walk alone
Over the dunes, drifting into the night.
With the wind and the waves and Your voice that saves,
You fill my darkness with Your light.

Glimmer

A soothing piano resonates in the quiet mood.
A river rolls along the stones beneath the night.
As I sit here with the one of whom I'm so fond,
Somewhere inside, I'm transported out and beyond.

The melody graces the shimmer of your flowing blond.
Tiny lamps along the wall are like pool lights
That waiver with the currents in the night.
The dark, marble counter draws the vague glimmer.

There's a message in the wordless moments,
When our breath and beating hearts unite us.
We wander along the golden strands
That stretch out between us like open hands.

For a moment, I can't help but stare into your eyes.
My uncasual gaze brings a blush to your lovely face.
I can't help but be caught by the light in your eyes,
Which brings your life before me with the love I feel inside.

I Gaze in Wonder

Ever since the day I first saw your face,
I've felt my life begin to change.
How could I have known, when I called you on the phone,
That your voice would make my heart sing your name?

Now, every time you're right here by my side,
I can't help but feel so amazed.
And I give thanks to God, that He's given me this time
To gaze into the beauty of your face.

And I gaze in wonder at all that I see,
When you're standing here before me.
As the moments go by like stars across the sky,
I'll use them all to show you mean the world to me.

I'll never forget the night you walked into my life;
Our paths crossed from across a crowded room.
First, there was the rain, and then the sun came.
And like a rose our love began to bloom!

As I gaze into your eyes, it's like an emerald sunrise—
Like the green that grows after the winter's snow.
And with every passing day, beyond all our words can say,
I know our love will only continue to grow.

And we gaze in wonder at the stars in the sky,
Like the shimmering silver on the sea.
Now, we're sailing out so far, beyond this sea of stars,
Sailing on the love between you and me.

In The Presence

Like a barren canvas
That awaits the brush of color,
This paper (so snowy white)
Invokes what hand and pen can offer.

Then, peering down like the first man,
Who in a pond saw his face—
These words peel back the layers,
Unveiling dreams that I still chase.

As I gaze in, I see
My own eyes looking back at me.
And I reflect upon the moments
Of the days that used to be.

Beyond the features of the landscape,
Above the tips of trees,
Clouds roll by across the sky,
Passing by the shaking leaves.

Then, my mind comes to rest at last
In the sky the clouds roll past.
And I'm in the presence of the One,
Who is the First and Last.

In This World

Billowing, white clouds paint pictures in the sky...
And you tell me what each one is, as it drifts slowly by.
As we sit out here watching the clouds,
There's no place that I'd rather be.
Now, I see your face in the morning light,
And a miracle is what I see!
As I watch you laugh and play
And see the wonder of life on your face,
I want to be there for you, as you make your way
Through the moments and stages of your days.
In this world, as you walk through your days,
There'll be challenges to face.
In this world, there's so much that I want you to see.
But, most of all, I want you to know the One,
Who'll always be there for you, like He's been there for me.

I Saw A Tree

I saw a tree, a live oak tree,
Growing by a bridge.
On a country road, a quiet, country road,
So towering within the sedge.

Peddling toward it upon my bike,
Its presence caught my eye.
I couldn't help but ponder that old tree,
As I went passing by.

It wasn't just any old oak tree.
I knew it had some stories to tell.
If it had the words, I knew it would
Paint the picture quite well!

A weathered tree it was, if I do say—
Its intricate branches against the sky.
If you hadn't a reason for gazing a while,
It could surely tell you why.

It could tell you of the sunrise
It beholds with each new day,
Or tales of all the many different folks
Who are passing on their way.

It could tell of endless showers of rain,

or when the days were cotton-mouthed dry.
It might recite a poem about the way the sun
Melts down at sunset beneath the summer sky.

This old fellow knows the night time stars so well.
He's watched as days have turned to nights...
have come and gone.
Like my circling tires or the creek that rambles by,
He knows the days will just keep rolling on.

Life's Just Begun

Wandering through morning clouds, sunlight finds its way
To the surface of the water where it undulates.
Our memories together flicker in my mind,
As I drift on reflections of another place and time.

We spent the summer nights pavilioned by the stars.
The diamonds in the sky unlocked the gateway of our hearts.
The universe expanded between you and me.
Like the blue in the sky, some things were meant to be.

In a sea of faces or from across the room,
Sometimes from a distance, I'll just pause and watch you.
Or, right here together, we'll sit so quietly.
There's just no way to capture how much you mean to me!

Now, as I think back to the way things used to be,
Our moments with each other flood my memory.
I just want to be with you every single day.
I'm so thankful that this love is here to stay.

I know that you were sent here from heaven to me.
The moonlight on your hair shines
Like the starlight on the sea.
There's a feeling about the moments—
So much of life has come and gone.
Then, I see you here beside me,
And it feels like life's just begun.

Moon

Down the staircase and out the door,
Georgia pauses for an instant on the lawn.
As a rush of breeze sweeps her blond hair into
A spray of scattered strands, skyward her eyes are drawn.

Torso swiveling into the headlong wind,
A luster glances off her pensive, saline eyes.
Downtrodden concerns swept away in midstream,
Her thoughts drift above the land into the boundless skies.

Trickling down from the night's expanse
And nestling on verdant petals and leaves,
Comes a mist of light streaming through the murk,
Whisking thoughts far away into the wonder it heaves.

Peering out from her shrouded soul,
She glimpses more than a glowing sliver.
She feels a presence in the dark, a breath of
Heaven in her heart— a hope of being delivered.

Only a crescent up there, suspended so high,
Reflecting rays from its own source of light.
But such a lodestar in the sky like a lighthouse by
The sea, it lights the course for vessels lost in the night.

When it exposes its full surface to the sun,
How much brighter it illuminates the sky.
How much more light, then, could our souls
Throw forth, if to Jesus we would fully draw nigh!

For now, the night lingers thick like paint,
As the earth whirls through space around the sun.
Muddled chatter mingles with a siren, squealing down a
Damp city lane, as laughter clumsily disguises desperation.

More than a Dream to Me

I've wandered along many moonlit shores,
Casting dreams into the sky.
I've prayed to God and done so much dreaming
About what He would do with my life.

Now, here I stand at the end of all my roads,
And I've stumbled and often lost my way.
I'd go through all of my sorrows again,
If it meant that I could be with you today.

Now, here we are, and I look in your eyes,
And I believe...
That God has given me more than I prayed for
Because you're more than a dream to me.

And with every passing moment,
I'll always be here for you.
All of my life and eternally,
I will always love you.

Through the trees, I gaze into the lake,
Which bears reflections of the sky.
I know God wants to reflect His glory
Through the love that brought us side by side.

So, darling, put your hand in mine,

As together we travel down this road.
May our love always reflect His glory,
Beyond tomorrow where the river flows.

Ocean Breeze

Search for me in the vacant moment,
When the world is at bay outside your door.
Feel my presence with the resounding waves
That soak in along the silent shore.

I follow the path of salty, weathered wood.
The ocean's sound is tunnel-like before me.
It resembles the 'Cuuwwssshhh' that you hear
With the spiraling conch shell pressed up to your ear.

In this room right by the sea,
I'm preparing a place for you and for me—
Somewhere out beyond this setting sun,
Where the seagulls float together as one.

I pause for an instant in the sudden stillness,
In the sunken valley between two sand dunes...
Between the wind, between two breaths of air...
Before this brimming basin, beneath a quarter moon.

The host of silent sea oats seem to sleep...
Their long, slender blades motionless, but alert.
Frozen for a small yet stretching span of time—
Then, they wave, knocking together like chimes.

It's a mystery; we can't foresee
Which ocean breeze will send a song to sing.

But we can prepare a place between you and me
For the love that will blow in off the sea.

(I pray it will one day blow in off the sea.)

Oh, Great Father, Lord to Me

Oh, Great Father, Lord to Me,
Draw me ever close to Thee.
Through the winds of changing days,
Let me ever seek Thy face.

Through the rain and snowy veil,
O'er the waves as I sail...
As I'm drifting o'er the lea,
Let me find my rest in Thee.

Oh, Great Father, Thy will be done.
Thank You for sending Christ Your only Son!
You are the Maker of heaven and earth.
You reached down in our darkness
And gave us a second birth.

Yours, the grapes upon the vine,
Aging water into wine,
Ripening apples on the tree—
All my blessings come from Thee!

Yours, the dew upon the grass—
In sunlight it fades so fast.
As the sun arcs o'er the sky,
Lead me as my days go by.

Oh, Great Father, Thy will be done.

Thank You for sending Christ, Your only Son!
When I consider the heavens
And the works of Thy hand,
Compared to all Thy glory,
Really, who is man?

With the brook that rambles by,
As birds soar o'er the sky...
From the mountains to the sea—
All of nature sings of Thee!

As wind rushes through the trees,
Hear the chorus of the leaves.
In the woods, I look to the sky.
I'll seek You as my days go by.

On the Waterfront

Sunlight sparkles on the waterfront like a
Sequined dress moving beneath the dance lights.
Beyond the boats, there's a steady stream of traffic
Crossing the bridge, just on the outskirts of sight.

By palmettos laced with a trace of Spanish moss,
I meander through grass, rich with dollar weeds.
A ship's silhouette floats on the horizon,
As a pod of pelicans glides by on the breeze.

The sprinkling salt shaker sound of cicadas
Blends with waves gently lapping against the bulkhead.
The saltwater breeze whispers softly,
Stirring a memory of something she said.

The ebbing, summer tide draws me far away,
Lost in reflections of another time.
Your voice resounds with the breaking waves.
Your Spirit calms me and gives deep peace inside.

Paul's Voyage to Take the Gospel to Rome

Sailing in an Alexandrian ship,
The sea billows swell beneath the heavy wind.
With the sounds of creaking masts and flapping sails,
The light of hope is flickering dim.

The Northeaster wind overtakes us,
And we're passed to the lee of an island by the storm.
They lower anchor for fear of the sandbars of Syrtis.
Our eyes are wild beneath the sky's dragon-like form!

The driving rain singes in a pellet-like fury!
The seamen tumble with the violently tossing boat.
Merciless, salty waves pound us and flood the deck.
Our voices are muted cries within our throats!

Battered violently day after day by the hurricane,
We throw cargo overboard to stay afloat in the sea's rage.
Neither sun nor stars appear for what seems a year.
We abandon all hope of being saved.

Drenched and languid, into a coma-like sleep I fall—
Where an angel of God intersects my helpless state.
He says to me, 'Fear not, Paul. The lives of all
Who sail with you will be saved by the God of grace.'

Though dense, ominous clouds still rain torrents,
And there's no safe port in view,
Peace and faith flood through my soul now
Because of the hand of God that will pull us through.

Pearls

I'm poised— not inclined
To pick up the driftwood anymore.
It still catches my eye, but even then...

Seashells are scattered here and there,
But most are just undesirable or broken
With no seaweed to cover the shattered edges.

Pier—
A fascination at night with its lights...
But, against this azure sky, dull as driftwood
Stretching out into the ocean.

How about the beach houses scattered about
Along this crescent-shaped island?
I've seen them splintered or uprooted by
Storm surge, only to float away in the sea.

Today, they look as cheap and flimsy
As strewn matchboxes upon the sand.

I meander onward down the shore—
A traveler... in a land of driftwood.

I saunter through wave-wet sand,
Leaving behind only vague footprints
That will soon be washed away.

The breakers fill me with a sense

Of my own incompatibility with time,
Which has me fading through an hour glass,
Born back, rowing against a sunset tide.

Each passerby seems to be fading along with me.

What are their treasures in this passing world?
Passing onward now, I'm drawn toward the pearls.

Rainbow

in the fury and haze of a tropical storm,
torrents of rain drench the earth.
the eye dismantles the helpless shore,
stirring up awe for this force without form.

the dark, massive, pregnant clouds loom;
they draw the curtain on the daylight.
rain patters on after the worst is through.
lightning flashes, and we wait for the boom.

rain pours down with heavy gusts of wind—
seems like it'll never let up.
drops of rain stream down in a frenzy!
dissipating darkness gives a hint of the end.

then, peering through the dark comes the blue;
it slowly devours the forboding sky.
the shower of rain dissolves into a drizzle.
atop the foliage, raindrops rest like dew.

on the margin of the tempest that still lingers,
i blink as a band of colors draws in my eyes.
i'm unleashed from my narrow perspective.
rays of light reach forth like God's own fingers!

only on the edge of the storm barely here
can the rainbow console with its brilliant display.

casting stars in our eyes, as we gaze through the sky,
though the storm's still here, hope drives out our fear.

Running beneath the Sun

Sprawling on a misty dawn in the city,
I feel the wake of things done and undone.
My heart longs to erase the clouds of the past,
As I run on the baked pavement beneath the sun.

Racing down the turning and twisting lanes,
I eye the rush of waves breaking ahead.
Cars and people rush by in incessant flashes.
I long to ease the rattling voices in my head.

I pass by the crumble of complexes,
As my legs bounce from the sugary sand.
In a new harmony, my lungs forget
The chaos of motion with its gripping demand.

The glimmering ocean reaches out toward me.
The gentle breeze shifts through my hair.
I feel the lifting presence of the Lord
Beneath the eyes of the sun and its blinding stare.

Seagulls gently lift above the white crests.
A white ship cuts into the horizon.
Patterns of fleecy clouds drift across the sky,
As I go running on.

Sea

Away from the things of man,
Beyond the silently swaying sea oats,
The tide drifts out to sea.

Just the trace of a gull's cry
And the gentle lap of tiny breakers
Are the sounds that come to me.

The rippled, powdery sand barely squeaks
Beneath my feet, as I walk toward the sound.
The sky puffs at my clothes.

I see a starfish washed ashore.
A battered shoe lies among scattered shells,
As I head down the coast.

Where the ocean meets the shore,
I watch the salty water wash over
A shell again and again.

The water engulfs the conch shell
And lets it go, trickling down through it
And sinking into the sand.

Far away on the breeze, there's a kite,
Pulled by a child near houses of white,
Adrift on the blue sky.

As I sit on the smooth beach,
I feel so much, yet so much fades away.
More than anything, I wish that I could stay.

Shadow of the Cross

i've been rendered listless by time's toll.
with nothing left to give, i wait— numb and still.
crushed in the wake of my sinfulness,
i'm given rays of light amid the mess.

I meander jagged like a vagabond,
strapped with a bit of nothing to give.
My bread, water, and two cent offerings
find their way to help a poor soul live.

A tangled web of dressed-up imperfection—
Dust to dust, yet I'm under renovation.
The Spirit sparks a fire inside to give.
There's so much more than for myself to live!

You lead me past the dead end of myself,
To repent, be restored, and sent back out.
You draw me off the well-worn paths
To meet with the needy and cast out.

In their eyes, I can see my reflection—
Just a beggar in the shadow of the cross.
Freely given Your undeserved mercy,
Beside the gift of Jesus, all else is loss!

On a littered corner of the street,
I see a man with a cardboard sign.

Wearing tattered jeans and a worn-out coat—
In his eyes, can you see the gaze of Christ?

Shadows of the Night

I was walking down the street last night,
Along a row of glowing streetlights
On a quiet city lane.

Looking into the starlit sky,
I began to remember the reason why
I was out here after all.

I was caught up in the scene,
Where nothing's what it seems.
In the shadows of the night,
I began to lose sight of my dreams.

Through the shadows of trees on the road,
I passed the houses down the row,
My shadow falling right behind.

In the moonlight, the rooftops were aglow.
With the light coming from the windows,
The lives inside were on my mind.

Are they caught up in the scene?
Where nothing's what it seems?
In the shadows of the night,
Are they losing sight of their dreams?

I will never forget the summer night

I was illumined in the Light
That began to lead me on!

At that moment I lost control,
And your Spirit took my soul
And led me where I'd never gone before.

Beneath a starless night,
You led me to the Light!
Now, my dreams are coming true,
As I keep my eyes on You.

As I travel down this wandering road,
I often wonder where I should go;
It isn't always very clear.

But You ask me to journey on
To the places that I've never gone.
You lead me, and I step out in faith.

Now, You're calling out to me,
Beyond all that I can see!
In the shadows of the night,
My dreams are taking flight.

Signatures of Infinity

Contemplating the far reaches
Of our mind-bending universe,
Distant galaxies and their stars
Are what I often dream of first.

Not suspended, but orbiting
Light years from our own, distant sun.
My thoughts then return to earth and
Our interstellar position.

From the rings encircling Saturn,
Way past the Halo Nebula,
God's left His mark on all He made
Like fingerprints all around us.

Through haunting endlessness of space,
God reached with love through all He'd made...
To send His Son to earth to die
And make a way beyond the grave!

Through the cry of soaring seagulls,
Over the breaking ocean waves,
The silver lining in the clouds
Sends down a band of harp string rays.

Every color of the sunset,
Over water and outstretched land,

It's an ever-changing painting—
Brushstrokes from Your eternal hand.

On every page of our story,
Within the scenes of what we see...
All of life is for His glory—
Signatures of Infinity.

Silver Curl

A tinge of coffee lingers on the tongue.
Dampness streaks through tangled strands of gold hair.
Metallic glare shoots by white-dotted lines.
Fusion of sun and cloud layers paint the air.

Unfolding from the vehicle in wobbly steps,
The guest welcomes the salt's full embrace.
Breaking fronts glide toward the shore.
Rays of light flicker from a squinted face.

Toes cringe with the chill of initial entry.
Ribs respond to the thrill of the board.
The glittering sheet peels out of the way,
As cupped hands like oars propel me forward.

Eyes that rivet with the incoming swells,
Trigger a release into the coming set.
I connect with the surging, silver curl,
Slicing down into the ride I'm about to get.

Moving with the wave, coiled into balance,
I rush with the sweep of the tide!
I flow with its surge as long as I can,
'Til it dissolves and brushes me aside.

Sun sets now where the ocean meets the sky.
I float lifelessly, bobbing with the sea.
The once-cluttered beach is almost vacant.
Today's packed up memories revisit me.

Details of all the rides are now but a haze,
But I vividly feel the essence in my soul,
Bleeding through my circuitry into my heart.
Invigorated spirit contrasts my body's loll.

Standing before the Mirror

Standing before the mirror,
His flaws gape wide open though out of view.
All he's held so dearly to is now mangled and diffused.

He glances at the t.v. and then the phone,
And the room suddenly seems in disarray.
His heart is the broken soil beneath the plow.
The knight's been slain in this tragic play.

In a car, he rolls along on tinted streets,
Hair swept in the evening's passing breeze.
As the lights of street lamps and cars slash by,
His soul leaps forward beyond the shadows of trees.

His cruising car unravels the mountain range,
And the views take his breath away.
Beneath an eternal ocean of stars,
His awed hush whispers what words can't say.

Across the cavernous valley that's sunken
Beneath an outstretched, everlasting sky,
He senses the weakening vortex of all the days gone by.

As he ponders the wreckage from his voyage,
He considers all that encircles him from far above.
As his countenance beholds the lofty heavens,
His heart is opened to eternal love!

As he stares into the inner ring

Of the expanse of stars and sky,
He sees a world of endless horizons
Upon the faith that God's awakened inside.

Stars

The stars seem to all but quiver
Above these streets tonight.
They offer such reflections
To the watchers of the night.

They've been known to stir the dreams
That toward heaven with wings do fly.
They compose a silent symphony
Draped out across the sky.

Waiting in such silence,
They gaze down from a canopy,
Amid the expanding dust cloud
That outlines the galaxy.

Like a sparkling mist
Over the world so dim and shadowy,
Peering in upon us,
Are they watching over me?

Stars of darkness, stars of light...
Cast out freely upon this pool of night.
Out above the world as far as we can see,
They bear reflections of eternity.

The stars seem to quiver
Above these streets tonight.

Maybe they feel the pressure to deliver
Something they can't give to the watchers of the night.

Sunrise on the Ocean

Rising in the early morning,
With some coffee, I head out on the pier.
I watch the waves break along the shore.
With the tides that rise and fall, I feel You here.

I cast my gaze down the island.
There's a silver lining in the clouds.
I'm slowly released from ebbing shadows,
As the Spirit sweeps out cobwebs of doubt.

With no nets to drag like a fishing boat,
I wait for a fish with this rod and reel.

As I squint out over the water,
Images and memories drift through my mind
And change the way I feel.

I cast my gaze along the coastline
To where cottages fade into the shore.
You've saved me and light the way to heaven.
How could I ever ask for anything more?

With this sunrise on the ocean,
You cast Your light into my soul—
Etching heaven's realities in scenes of clouds,
Calling me to envision distant streets of gold.

Swedish Winter

Through a thousand miles of winter darkness,
Far above the crystal-covered forests of pine,
You've lit a canopy of candles,
Giving the stars the light to shine.

Down below a ceiling of shimmering ice,
The fish in the lake through darkness, slowly glide...
Out past the tall, ice-covered sedge,
Which is rooted in the soil at the water's edge.

On the fringe of the frozen forest,
I spot a doe with her young by her side.
Looking in their starlit eyes, I think about
Our God who made them and keeps them alive.

I feel Your hand in the Swedish winter,
Though days are a snow cloud's breath and nights are long.
Lead me with Your divine direction
And fill me with Your love like a heavenly song.

Swimming within Me

The anemone waves at me,
As I submerge further now into the deep.
Swimming within me and now surfacing
Are visions from dreams when I've been asleep.

I'm in a colony of living things,
Vibrant and moving about in their world
Down here, nestled about this coral reef.
Emerging thoughts of the supernatural swirl.

Upon the rocks and shells, alien-looking
Sea plants and jelly anemone haunt me.
An orange starfish lies alone on the sand,
As I skim along the floor of the sea.

I dislodge a sea urchin from the rocks
Carefully, so it doesn't make me bleed.
I inspect and then wiggle its black needles,
As a school of glimmering fish dash by me.

All the sounds I hear swim to me in slow motion,
Engulfed by liquid. I hear a low-pitched hum;
It's from the motor of a distant boat cutting by.
I float amid rising sand particles that glitter in the sun.

I swivel my head slowly from left to right
And notice the prune-like skin on my fingertips.
I push down sharply with my hands as if to fly.
I rise with the bubbles all around me and then float a bit.

I hover down and stare off toward the distant ocean depths
That stretch endlessly into the darkness of the unknown.
My mind floods with thoughts of this engulfing enormity,
Which coats across thousands of miles far from home.

Fins in hand on the shore, I walk away from the sea.
The sun melts upon the water along with the day.
I take one last glance at the ocean and turn to go,
Leaving only footprints— soon to be washed away.

Tangerine Sunset

As the tangerine sunset slowly swallows a flamingo,
My angst glides down a glossy, sedge leaf
And forms into a dangling droplet,
Which clings to this perilous vantage by its teeth.

But, lo, the gravity has its sway,
And the protuberant sphere of rainwater
Submits and plummets to the earth,
Humbly absorbed into its maker.

The decomposing of my melancholy
Scrapes the dust off of my awareness.
The cosmic rolls up the sleeves of chaos,
Seeping through the veneer of nature.

A divine ripple touches to the fringes of the moors.
Yesterday... today... forever...
— Ever lending transformation, yet transcending
The grip of this alteration itself.

10,000 Years

Before the existence of anything,
Out of nothing–You brought life to be.
You're the beginning and the end of it all.
You roll the sky right into the sea.

Oh, Creator of heaven and earth,
You spun the fabric of the universe.
Long before You brought us into this world,
You made the way to our salvation first!

Before the foundation of the world,
You chose Christ to die in my place.
You save us not by deeds that we've done,
But for Your plan by redeeming grace.

I was a grain of sand on the seashore, yet
Your Son breathed life into a dead castaway!
I was lost on the far end of the universe;
Now, to the gates of paradise, You lead the way.

One day, He'll descend through the clouds
On a white horse, His eyes burning like a flame!
He'll rule the nations with an iron rod forever.
The Word of God is His name!

Ten thousand years will come and go, and
Our days in heaven will have only just begun.

With multitudes of angels, we'll worship Jesus
In the awesome presence of God's own Son!

There, we'll glorify God on His throne,
Encircled in a rainbow by a crystal sea.
Lightning strikes and peals of thunder!
We'll be together in heaven eternally.

The Ballerina

Images flash through the dancer's mind,
As she imagines every move she'll make.
Her nerves are like electric wires,
But that's the pressure she's learned to take.

Heart rates quicken! Whispered voices grow tense,
As the crowd eyes the poised dancer's frozen stance.
Adrenaline surges through this static moment;
Even time seems to stand still for the dance.

Shattering the suspense with one gesture,
The ballerina springs into motion!
The patterns of her graceful movement
Are like the soothing rhythms of the ocean.

Tantalizing the crowd with allegro,
Bouncing in harmony with the song,
All the repetition and rehearsal
Lends to breathtaking, effortless ballon.

Pausing from a sequence of point work,
She pirouettes into the open space—
Stepping and gliding with virtuoso,
Choreography rendered with grace.

Every body part is so neatly arranged.

With each motion, her muscles are in sync.
Every delicate move is spontaneous
Because out here there's no time to think.

She soars with bravura across the stage,
Captivating all eyes within this place.
Each move flows so easily now, as
The trace of a smile lights her snow-white face.

The crowd applauds the dancer's performance,
As she curtseys in reply.
She will savor this moment forever,
For tonight she was like a star in the sky.

The Coming of Sleep

As I slip into that subterranean world,
What dreams may come...
When consciousness gives way to the subconscious tide
That sweeps o'er the inner eye...

Like the wind that rushes over the fields of Kansas,
Rolling patterns of clouds across the sky.
No one knows when it will come or
Where it's going, but it will keep blowing.

Streams of thought give birth to celestial utterances,
Their supple sprouts overtaking this fertile soil.
My capsule detaches from its gravitational moorings,
And the world retracts with this ascent into space.

Ears ring in the dark in the absence of sound.
Shallow breaths recede, as deep ones cover me.
My mind at rest begins to escape to another place,
But I'm unaware when, at last, it wiggles free.

The Divot upon the Pervading Darkness

The candlelight disperses the mask of black
Like a divot upon the pervading darkness.
A little pocket where the myths are dispelled,
Even while they grow on past the edges.

I can hear the vague echo of dissolution,
Perched here with a side-glance vantage.
Through a window pane, I see tree limbs trembling,
Twisted and crooked against the billowing sky...

Etching shadows upon old churches
And buildings, as they branch out over the ground.
Branch shadows quiver with light gusts of wind,
Which drag old, fallen leaves across the ground.

Some swirl about for an instant
And then come to rest against worn gravestones.
Through wispy clouds, a sliver of moon
Barely illumines the night and those graves.

The hard, dark soil is contoured with roots
Emanating from the systems of giant trees.
As the whispering wind stirs their leaves,
I ponder how they congregate down deep.

Stretching down through the darkness of sod,

They bring sustenance to those living trees.
Deep down, they drink water and find their bed,
Intermingling with the living and the dead.

The Frog Symphony

The frog symphony echoes in the dark.
Croaking rings out past the silhouettes of trees.
Sampling wine on this summer night,
I'm a ship on a distant sea.

For so long, down a series of hallways,
I've searched for an open door.
Here, I find peace away from the past
Like waves lapping onto the silent shore.

Above beds with needles of pine,
Through patches of hanging leaves,
Illumined in the light of the moon,
The breeze shifts through shadows of trees.

It carries the faraway sound of a train's whistle
Through a silence that was before...
Echoing over roofs and chimneys
Towards a quietly waiting door.

Fireflies flash faintly in a cove.
I embrace the moment here around me.
Your grace lifts my spirit beyond the fray
To a place where I know I'm free.

The Gift

Turn your eyes from the glamour and show—
From the lights, the lies, and things of gold.
For a moment, reject the allure of the world
And reflect on a story we need to be told.

A King was born a pauper in a lonely town,
Though His true residence is a lofty throne.
A Shepherd on a hillside watching His flock—
He leads home the ones God calls His own.

Briefly vacating His place in heaven from
Eternity past (before time existed at all),
Jesus—God in flesh—entered the world,
Born an infant in the mire of a cattle stall.

He came not for wealth or human approval,
Or to claim an earthly, temporal crown.
Jesus came to endure the horrific cross
And bring redemption with His blood that ran down!

Long before the first snow had drifted down,
Or the earth's foundations had been laid,
God chose the gift of His atoning Son
To cause the ones He calls to be saved.

His crucified, dead body was laid in a cave,
But three days later the stone was rolled away!

He appeared on earth for forty more days,
As proof He'd conquered sin and the grave!

Today, near Jerusalem is an empty tomb.
His body wasn't found because He's alive!
He's now exalted in heaven and will return
To take the redeemed to worship at His side.

the illusion

...Gradually, the self-constructed illusion
had worn thin... the one I meticulously crafted
in futility ever since we first met... reflexive
embellishments, pretense, and cover-ups
wove themselves into the very fabric
of our initial conversations... like
an elaborate, yet flimsily-constructed disguise...
a child's craft project that won't quite hold together.

Or like the striking painting you see
from across the room with a myriad
of brilliant colors and lavish brushstrokes...
as it draws you closer, passing by the mirrors,
you notice a seemingly growing number
of imperfections and spiderwebbed cracks
across the textured paint... as well as
noticeable flaws in the canvas itself...
it's hard to wipe them from the fringes of your mind,
as you retreat from its view...
while most of the initial (and somehow enduring)
qualities of attraction seem vaguely marred by
those foundational imperfections...

Then, sitting in the cool, leather chair
late that night in our living room, just beyond
the looming light fixture in the foyer, I felt myself
slowly letting go of the incessant compulsion

to do damage control of the minutia
and the mundane... suddenly, I'm aware
that the delusions have mostly unraveled...

And what we're left with, we embrace
even more than what was there before...
beyond the superficial layers
that we'd so meticulously draped
over the substance of who we really are...

The Ocean of Your Eyes

Long before I'd ever met you,
Sometimes my thoughts would drift away.
All alone beneath a sea of stars,
I'd dream of meeting you some day.

I'd often say a prayer for you,
Before I even knew your name.
Then, one day you walked into my life,
And my heart will never be the same.

Now, here we are together tonight
Beneath the diamonds in the sky.
My heart is sailing past the horizon
Across the ocean of your eyes.

Looking back on our memories together,
If I could, I'd do it all again.
But I'd rather be right here with you now
Than any place that we've ever been.

And now I often pray for you,
And I thank our God above,
Who connects our hearts together
Through His eternal love.

And here we are together tonight

Beneath the diamonds in the sky.
My heart is sailing past the horizon
Across the ocean of your eyes.

And with every dawn that fills the morning sky,
I praise the One who sent you
To be right here by my side.

The Place Where You Are

Been out here for such a long, long time
Traveling down this lonesome road.
I've seen a million miles come between us...
Watched the trees turn from green to gold.

The shifting seasons have changed the landscapes
All around us and within.
For now, I'd rather be right here with you
Than revisit the places that we've been.

The fields roll by outside my window
Like the days before me and the times gone by.
Through all the sounds of the world around me,
I'll always hear the still, small voice right by my side.

And it takes so much to say it now,
But the distance has gone too far.
I've got to find a way to get back
To the place where you are.

And now, I'm traveling out
Beyond all the darkness in me.
Then, suddenly, I see! My God,
You are all that I need.

The Pond's Surface

The pond's surface is illumined by the sun.
My eyes are brightened by that jetting light
Across this wavering mirror surrounded by pines.
The girl on the other bank snaps twigs one by one,
Setting some adrift. Finding my own stick,
With a gentle prod, I set it on its course
To float on out, bobbing with each ripple's force.
Suddenly, it slows not moving a lick.
Then, the bristling pines begin to sway.
And, after a delay, the stick takes another path
With the breeze like a sailboat skirting past.
I think about my life sailing on its way,
Responding to the winds of the Holy Ghost.
Without His leading, I'd be stagnant by the coast.

There is a Fire

There is a fire that won't be consumed,
Made for those not saved by God's grace.
Horrific and eternal, with screams that won't end,
There is no exit to get out of this place.
The stairway to heaven built with good deeds
Leads them straight to these infinite flames.
Jesus warned that this fire is unquenched.
The Lamb's book of life doesn't have their names.
Dead in transgressions, now they're here,
Punished with the father of every lie.
No mercy— just weeping and gnashing of teeth!
And the worms that eat them don't die!
There is a fire that won't be consumed.
Oh, crackle of flames and endless hissing!
In the Bible, Jesus speaks of these horrors,
Where human agony and torment is eternal.
Will they imagine heaven eternally,
And what they'll be forever missing?

These Days

Fragments of fleeting moments,
Seemingly disconnected in time,
Are somehow interwoven in
A collection of all the days gone by.
These memories across time's canvas,
Some faint and others are bright,
Draw the mind so far away
Like a ship's distant, blinking light.

All of these memories are
Like waves that wash into the shore,
Flowing in with the tide...
Receding to where they were before.
These days keep passing us by,
As we're walking along the sand.
In this world, I'm just passing through, too.
And I know my time is in God's hands.

I take another look at the boats on the water,
As I walk along the coast.
I stop to pick up fragments and shells,
Gathering the things that matter most.
My eyes follow a trail of seagulls,
Drifting into the setting sun.
The light on another day is fading slowly,
And soon I'll be heading home.

The Tide

The tide rises and falls inside my veins.
No two, frothy waves kiss my shores the same.
Your light sparkles like the constellations in me.
My nerves shimmer like golden nets on moonlit seas.

The ocean's magnetic chest heaves paternally.
The dark, rippling liquid runs its fingers along the beach.
Phosphorescent reflections of shore lights
Allude to lost ships and concealed treasures beyond reach.

Like a white marlin dragged in on a weighted net,
I'm caught by this black abyss of sea.
Tonight this vast deep would leave Coleridge's mariner
Without a rhyme, tossing in his sleep.

From my watch at the weathered, Cliffhouse wall,
The hissing, salty surge surrounds the rocks below.
Pale fog slithers forth on the horizon like a ghost;
I watch it creep closer and closer to the coast...

The Traveler

The buzz of cicadas along the road
Rings out and fills the night air.
As I drive into the setting sun,
The summer twilight washes away all care.

My mind returns to the peace of the coast
Where breakers filled my senses all day.
Now, as I roll along by rows of cornstalks,
I can't help but think, "I'm glad I came this way."

As the sun sinks low, replays of images
Flash like dreams across the windshield of my mind.
Passing by the groves and rows of tobacco,
I'm a traveler through the fields of time.

My speed makes the warm, salty air feel cooler.
I can still taste salt from the ocean near my lips.
Browsing through a collection of ocean shells,
I revisit memories of past beach trips.

I still feel ripples of waves from the past,
Flowing on towards tomorrow, wind across the mast.
My heart's echo is in the gull's cry—
On the breeze, ever learning to fly.

The Wings of Grace

When everything is quiet,
I let my mind drift away.
And, suddenly, I'm at peace.
And the troubles of this world fade away.

Even when the rain is pouring in my face,
And everything seems so out of place—
Through it all as we run this race,
I know You're gonna lift us up on the wings of grace.

Somewhere... even before I say a prayer—
Though I cannot see Your face,
I know You are there.
(I know You are there.)

Through this old world,
As we're traveling down this road,
Passing through these stages of life,
We've all got such a long way to go.

Even when shadows block the sunlight from my face,
When I just can't seem to find my place...
Through it all, as I run this race—
I know God's gonna lift me up on the wings of grace.

Though I Can't Tell You Now

Here we are tonight in the candlelight,
And you're sampling soothing melodies.
Your guitar in the soft, low light
Stirs my heart and mind to poetry.

Penning words into meter and rhyme,
I've done through the years thousands of times.
Now, I see you there with your golden hair,
And no language can capture what I feel for you.

With every beat of my heart, we're becoming a part
Of each other with every new day.
Like the candles that glow around the room,
My heart just melts when I'm with you.

The beauty of your eyes is like the starlit skies
That seem to bring heaven into view.
I can see how heaven must be
Because I feel it when I'm right here with you!

Though I can't tell you now,
The depths of how much I feel for you,
I'll take all of my life with you as my wife
To show you how much I love you.

Traces in My Mind

Right on the edge of the limits of sight,
A tiny airplane arches over the sky...
Etching a pathway across the stratosphere,
Before the day gives way to the night.

A shimmering vapor trail across the sky,
Silver and gold in the afternoon sun,
Leaves its traces far above the world,
Before another day is done.

Cutting a passageway through a pillar of clouds,
Over the water and the fields, so far down—
Up here the constant change of life is suspended,
And then affirmed with every passing cloud.

So many moments have come and gone,
Leaving traces of their presence in my mind.
So, I'll just sit out here and soak it in for a while,
Before another comes and drifts on by.

Visions in the Reflections

Traveling along this path of life,
Sometimes this second is all I can see.
Then, suddenly, time just slips on by.
The moments fade into a memory.

I watch the rise and fall of the oceans...
The drifting pelicans that come and go.
The times with you along these shores
Are treasures I'll savor beyond tomorrow.

Drifting on the tides of a lifetime,
Beneath the phases of the distant moon,
We fly on the rhythms of the clouds
To a tomorrow that's coming so soon.

We've journeyed down such different paths,
As far as the land of the midnight sun.
All the while, God was building a bridge between us,
And now our roads have become as one.

Now, looking back, I'm sifting
Through the pages of yesterday.
There are visions in these reflections
That help us savor where we are today.

Walking through the Pages

Sifting through the pages
Composed on scrolls so long ago,
I'm lost in this unfolding story.
Through every word, God speaks to my soul.

I read of a Man who walked a lonely road—
Called to outcasts, sinners, the destitute.
He healed the sick and wept with those who cried.
He was rejected, though He spoke the words of Truth.

Walking through the pages, promised through the ages,
He walked through the sands of time...
To walk along the sands of our shores.
His name is Jesus Christ. He is Lord!

He was despised by the religious authorities,
Until they nailed Him on a cross at Calvary.
At the Place of the Skull, He bore our transgressions.
The sinless bled and died for sinners on that tree.

Before His birth in a manger,
In the inn there was no room.
After thirty-three years of giving so much to others,
He was given a tomb.

But on the third day, the women were afraid;
The tombstone was rolled away!
The angel said, "He is risen!
Come see the place where He lay."

On the road to Emmaus, He appeared to them.
He showed Thomas the nail holes in His hands.
To fulfill the words and prophecies of Scripture,
The gift of Jesus was God's plan!

Through every season of life,
He always shows me something new.
Through the books and letters written by the Holy Spirit,
I surrender to Your Truth!

Walking through the pages, promised through the ages,
He walked through the sands of time...
To walk along the sands of our shores.
His name is Jesus Christ. He is Lord!

Walk through Scenes

They resonate and come back again—
These stories from the days of yesteryear.
Gravitating towards the evening hours,
On reminiscent thoughts, they'll drift near.

Somewhere out of a memory,
In a low-lit scene on a quiet night,
These stories draw out our wistful tones,
As they drift back in the fading light.

Revisited across the channels of time,
Those moments take on different shades of light.
They recede again, as time moves on by,
Like the wind through the fields in the night.

Beneath a canopy of trees,
We walk through scenes of the days gone by,
As a blinking plane's light makes its way
Across the endless summer sky.

Wither Wilt I Go

Wither wilt I go?
Only God could ever know
Which way the wind will blow.
While inclement weather wilted the willows,
I wonder which plant will profit most
From the weeping billows on the wind.
The wind is weeping,
While the raindrops on the window
Lend for good sleeping!
In the silence of my room,
I wander through a world of dreams,
Between the seams... in surreal scenes,
Where nothing is what it seems.
With visions and revisions, my mind teems.
Like a whirlwind, off the deep end
In waterfall formation,
The subconscious mind transcends
What the waking eye comprehends
Through such a narrow lens.
As the sedated (yet animated) mind ascends
(or maybe descends?) within,
Around   each   bend,
The images that synapses send
blend... and lend   a   new spin
Without any foreseeable   end.
If, in a flash, it all were to end,
It would be beyond what one

Could comprehend about the future.
What can be foreseen in a dream?
Left to itself, it cannot portend.
Mostly, it can only pretend to know
How to impress a possible way to go.
Through the weeping willows,
The wind continues to blow.

With Tears in Our Eyes

A salt-laden wind presses against our bodies,
As, beneath the overcast eve, we walk together.
As we pass beneath the pier, I take your hand in mine,
Glancing at the damp pilings shimm'ring down the line.
Looking out towards the indistinguishable skyline,
We hear the wordless whispers on the waterfront.
As waves rush over our feet and spread along the shore,
I feel you here beside me like I never have before.
The breeze wafts at the waves in your blond hair,
And we begin to speak the words we've meant to say—
Their truth long elusive to our tear-filled eyes.
Pain and joy flow mingled down from stars piercing the sky.
Our toes sink further into our seat in the grains,
And our tears become as one in our embrace.
I can feel you streaming through me,
As the world around us fades away.

With the Seabirds and My Kids

The emerald tide washes along the shore,
As I sit listening quietly to its rhythmic roar.
With the seabirds and my kids, I spend the day,
Finding such joy just watching them play.

Sand toys and shells are tossed beside my chair.
Scent of salt and the gulls' cry fill the air.
As the wind shifts through Georgia's blond hair strands,
Sand and time sifts through her tiny hands.

Harrison is building a fort of sand and shells.
Emma Claire is dancing near the rolling swells.
The tide washes away time for a while,
And I see the world through the eyes of a child.

Could someone say the words to me —
That I'll never lose sight of these memories?
Or promise by some miracle far from now,
I can revisit these moments somehow?

Oh, God, when these times have ebbed away,
Help my mind's eye still see this scene today.
When the sun sets on what we have here,
I pray You'll draw these memories near.

You are the One

I could never tell you all the things
That you are to me.
You are the water inside my sea.

And every time I think about you,
My feelings run so deep...
Way past the roots of any 300-year-old tree.

And every time I write about you,
The ink runs off the page.
My love for you is far beyond where any words can reach.

You are the one
I've been waiting on for so long.
When we're together, my heart wells up in song!

Every time I look into your eyes,
All my shadows fade away.
Right here in your arms is where I want to stay.

Like a bonfire on the beach,
My heart burns for you.
You make the bleakest of my winter skies turn blue.

Lying in your arms, sometimes
My tears fall on your face because
You take my heart to such a heavenly place!

How beautiful you are to me!

Everything about you is so lovely.
You are a rose in the valley.
I will love you to the end of eternity.

Your Grace

Planes trace distant trails like wind socks
Above lines of clouds painted in the sky.
My fishing line flitters in the ocean breeze,
As a pod of pelicans sleekly whisks by.

The fishing boat trawls, buoyed by waves.
Traces of seagulls hover above the nets.
Gratitude covers me like this sunscreen
And washes away yesterday's regrets.

But Your grace goes so much deeper
Than any feelings that I have today.
The salvation that You've given me—
No ocean could wash away.

As my faith shifts like grains of sand,
Set my soul on the rock of grace.
Long before You brought me into this world,
You chose your Son to die in my place!

A mountain stream trickles through the woods,
Rolling gently over mossy, green stones.
The trees filter sunlight on the forest floor.
Smoke rises from the chimney of a distant home.

You draw my eyes to a painting in the sky—
The colors brushed with the setting sun.

Its movement whispers of time and heaven,
As the light fades on another day that's done.

Made in the USA
Middletown, DE
05 November 2023